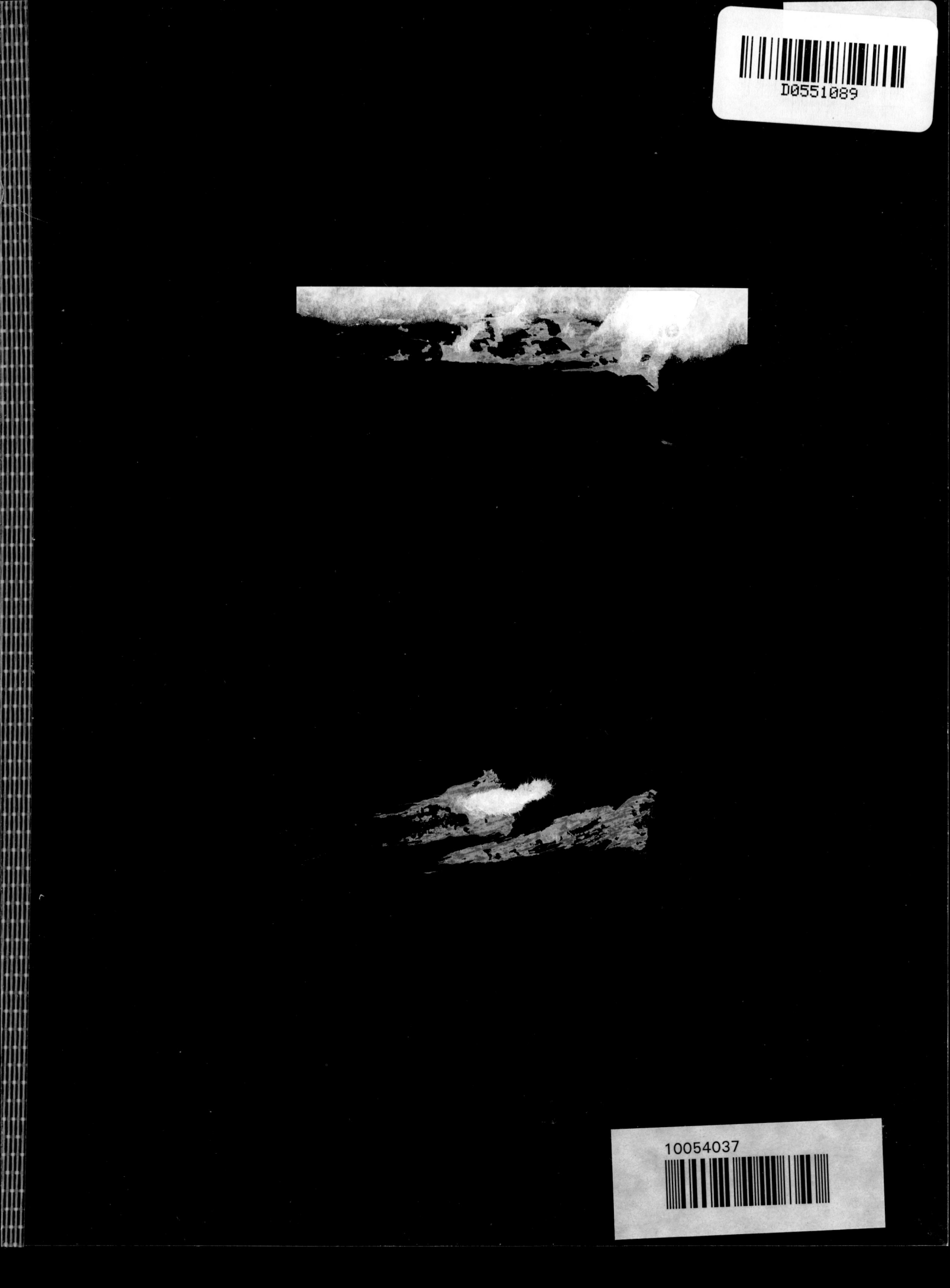

20TH CENTURY MEDIA

1990s
ELECTRONIC MEDIA

20TH CENTURY MEDIA – 1990s
was produced by

David West 🏃 Children's Books
7 Princeton Court
55 Felsham Road
London SW15 1AZ

Picture Research: Carrie Haines
Designer: Rob Shone
Editor: James Pickering

First published in Great Britain in 2002 by
Heinemann Library, Halley Court, Jordan Hill,
Oxford OX2 8EJ, a division of Reed Educational and
Professional Publishing Limited.

OXFORD MELBOURNE AUCKLAND
JOHANNESBURG BLANTYRE GABORONE
IBADAN PORTSMOUTH (NH) USA CHICAGO

Copyright © 2002 David West Children's Books

06 05 04 03 02
10 9 8 7 6 5 4 3 2 1

ISBN 0 431 15260 8 (HB)
ISBN 0 431 15274 8 (PB)

British Library Cataloguing in Publication Data

Parker, Steve, 1952-
20th century media 1990s: electronic media
1. Digital media - History - Juvenile literature
I. Title II. Twentieth-century media 1990s
302.2'34'09048

Printed and bound in Italy

PHOTO CREDITS :
Abbreviations: t-top, m-middle, b-bottom, r-right,
l-left.

Cover, 4b, 6, 7tr & m, 9tr & br, 11ml, 12t, 13tl, 14r,
14-15t, 15tr, 16bl & tr, 17r & b, 18tr, 19mr, 20b, 23bl
& br, 24-25b, 25b, 28 all - Popperfoto/Reuters. Cover
bl - NASA. 3, 5mr, 8tl - Corbis Stock Market. 4-5, 9tl
- Courtesy Apple Macintosh. 5t, 20tl, 21t, br & bl,
22br, 22-23t, 23tr - The Kobal Collection. 5bl, 8br,
17tl, 26bl, 27m - BSkyB. 7bl & br, 10bl - Rex
Features. 15br - The Defence Picture Library. 18b -
Topham Picturepoint. 24tl - (Giovanni De Bei), 25mr
(Kieran Doherty) - Redferns. 25tl - Dave Benett @
Alpha London. 26-27b - Popperfoto. 26-27 & 27t -
Castrol. 29tr - Press Association/Topham Picturepoint.

*The dates in brackets after a person's name
give the years that he or she lived.*

*An explanation of difficult words can be
found in the glossary on page 30.*

20TH CENTURY MEDIA

1990s
ELECTRONIC MEDIA

Steve Parker

Heinemann
LIBRARY

CONTENTS

10054037
302.23

NEWEST AND BIGGEST
5

FREE AT LAST
6

DIGITAL FUTURE
8

TOO MUCH TV?
10

THE NET SPREADS
12

UNCONTROLLABLE
14

INSTANT NEWS
16

STORED FOREVER
18

VIRTUAL MOVIES
20

WORLD CINEMA
22

MUSICAL DREAMS
24

MEDIA MEET SPORT
26

INTO THE NEW MILLENNIUM
28

GLOSSARY & TIMELINE
30

INDEX
32

DOORWAY TO THE E-WORLD

The mouse is like a door handle, and its computer the door, into a separate universe – the Internet. Computers continued to become faster and more powerful during the '90s, and took over some of the roles previously filled by TV, video and records.

INTER-NERDS

The Internet could allow anyone anywhere to find out anything, via a computer and phone link. Journalists use it as an ideal medium to get news stories to a global public in seconds. But might the 'Net' spawn a generation of nerds who experience life only through their screens and speakers?

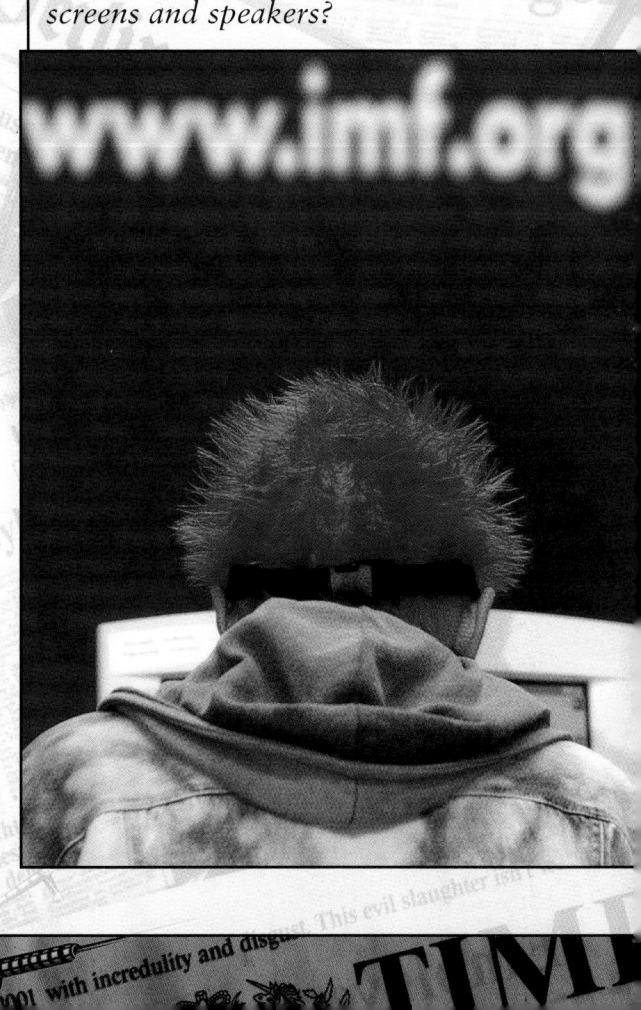

NEWEST AND BIGGEST

MOVIES
The medium of cinema was overwhelmed by a tidal wave of special effects. But did they guarantee success? No.

TOO MUCH OF NOTHING
Digital TV has bought hundreds of new 24-hour channels. But still people complain: 'there's nothing on'.

We find out news, views, information and knowledge through the media. At the start of the 20th century the main medium for news and entertainment was print – words and pictures, in newspapers and books. There were also visual media, like painting, and performance media, such as theatre. Then came movies, recorded sound, radio, terrestrial television, satellite and cable TV, video, CDs, DVDs and many other media formats.

'TEXT ME'
During the '90s, more mobile phones and masts offered the new communication medium of the text message.

Media experts made an amazing calculation at the end of the 20th century. More words and pictures had been made available to the public in its last four years, than in the rest of the 20th century – and in all the centuries before. This is due to the awesome growth and power of the Internet. In the 21st century, where will this amazing new medium take us?

FREE AT LAST

Some saw him as a freedom-fighter. To others he was a terrorist. He was held in prison for 27 years, on the crime of trying to overthrow the government by sabotage. No pictures of him were allowed during this period. Then in 1990 he appeared on global television, released at last. Four years later he was president of his newly united nation.

'FREE NELSON'

Nelson Mandela (born 1918) grew up in the Transkei region of South Africa, and studied law at Johannesburg. In 1944, he joined the ANC (African National Congress), a group dedicated to gaining equal rights for all people in South Africa. At the time, only white people had full rights, under a racist system known as apartheid. Mandela was jailed for his part in disruptive sabotage campaigns to destroy targets such as electricity pylons.

HELLO AGAIN
Photographs of Mandela were banned during his long years in prison. His release, here with wife Winnie, generated intense excitement – partly to see what he now looked like. The 1960s South African government had regarded his acts as terrorism. But to people who believed in freedom for all, not just for those of a certain race or skin colour, Nelson Mandela's actions were for a just cause.

6

RELEASE DAY

The anti-apartheid struggle went on. It encompassed many media: news and reports in the papers, on TV and radio, and powerful works of music, poetry, drama and visual arts. At last, South Africa's white-elected government, led by F. W. de Klerk, recognized a need for change. On 11 February 1990, Mandela walked out of Victor Verster Prison near Cape Town, into a media frenzy. It was the first time he had been seen in public since 1962.

A NEW ERA

Mandela had lost none of his burning desire to gain justice and freedom for all citizens. In 1994, South Africa held its first election where any adult, regardless of colour, could vote. The ANC triumphed and Mandela became president. Again, the world's media and public were captivated with awe and respect. Mandela had the best-known face on the planet.

LAWYER
Mandela worked as a lawyer during the 1950s, trying to defeat apartheid by peaceful means.

SYMBOLIC SHAKE
Mandela and de Klerk, both lawyers, greatly respected each other. De Klerk became South Africa's second deputy president.

CELEBRATION

In the medium of popular music, many singers and musicians campaigned and wrote songs against the apartheid system in South Africa. In March 1990, only a month after Mandela's release, a massive concert was held in his honour in London. When Mandela appeared as special guest, the crowd went wild.

MAJORITY RULE
The South African elections of May '94 were covered in great detail by news media.

Wembley Stadium, London, 1990.

DIGITAL FUTURE

Digits are numbers: 1, 2, 3 and so on. Digital systems are those based on numbers. Information such as words, pictures or sounds are represented as codes of numbers. Why is this so good, and how has it affected the media?

TOWER POWER
Masts for mobile phones sprang up like giant weeds.

SMALLER, BIGGER
The year 2000 mobile phone was one-tenth the size of the 1990 version. G3 (third generation) mobiles promised Internet access via the on-screen display.

DIGITAL VERSUS ANALOGUE

Computers are digital. In fact their binary system has only two digits: 1 (a short pulse of electricity) and 0 (no pulse). All information, instructions, programs and data in a computer are in the form of billions of these binary digits, or 'bits'. Compact discs and DVDs are digital too. But the broadcast media of radio and television began before digital technology was advanced. They were analogue, as were audio and video cassettes, and most telephones. Their signals are coded in the form of waves that vary continuously up and down.

DONE BY NUMBERS

BOX ON THE BOX
Some decoder boxes receive TV broadcasts in digital form, and convert them into analogue signals for the traditional TV set. This saves buying a new digital TV set – for now.

During the '90s, radio and TV began the switch to digital. The signals were sent out, not as waves, but as ultra-fast streams of on-off digital pulses. Between three and ten times as many TV or radio channels can be squeezed into the batch of signals used for one analogue channel. This allows more programmes and choices. Digital is higher quality, making sounds clearer and pictures sharper. It's also less prone to error, so information is transferred almost perfectly from one form to another as it passes through the broadcasting system.

FLAT SCREENS
A normal TV has a bulky, heavy glass 'tube'. 1990s advances in liquid-crystal technology made flat screens just as bright and clear.

SIDE BY SIDE

Digital data such as pictures and sounds can be stored on CD/DVD, and fed directly into a computer, to be manipulated. By the year 2000, digital TV and radio were making some impact. But people were wary. Would expensive digital equipment be another 'fad', quickly overtaken by yet further advances? Many countries decided to wait and see, and run digital and analogue media side by side.

THE 'PET' COMPUTER

In 1998 Apple computers began a new design trend with their curvaceous, colourful, easy-to-use iMac (internet Macintosh). It was marketed less as a boring-looking work tool, and more as a fashion accessory and friendly personal 'pet'.

SHRINKING WORLD

Smaller 'chips' and other devices meant that radios, phones, computers and other electronic media equipment shrank through the decade. Desktop became laptop, then laptop became palmtop, to sit on your hand. PDAs (personal digital assistants) acted as diaries and notebooks, and allowed basic computing functions on the move, to feed into the main computer back at base.

A 1997 digital car radio.

TOO MUCH TV?

Terrestrial, satellite, cable, analogue and digital, new programmes, endless repeats, dozens of stations, hundreds of channels, local and national, 24-hour broadcasting, on-demand movies, recordings on videotape and DVD, interactivity – the world's number one medium has it all. Can people really still complain that there's 'nothing on TV'?

MORE CHOICE

The digital revolution (see page 8) allowed more TV channels and programmes then ever before. Some of the extra 'capacity' – the ability to carry more and more information – was taken up by wider consumer choice. For one programme, such as a sports match, the viewer could choose which camera angles to see, which slow-motion replays to watch, and the language for the commentary. In the UK, the BSkyB satellite company captured many prominent sporting fixtures from 'free-to-air' BBC and ITV. People had to pay to view them. Pay-TV was expected to spread in the new millennium.

BIG-MONEY PRIZES
Quiz and game shows, very popular in the 1950s, came back big-time with massive cash prizes. Each had special features, like phone-a-friend on the UK's Who Wants to be a Millionaire? with Chris Tarrant.

LESS CHOICE

The glut of TV feasting did not extend around the world. The most populated nation, China, had a single major organization, CCTV (China Central Television). This ran about 10 channels, some broadcasting just a few hours each day, and all under strict control of the communist state authorities.

KIDS' TV

Specialist children's shows and channels continued to expand. Would too much TV make kids pale and weak? This debate dates back 50 years.

REALITY TV?

Contestants on Big Brother *were isolated from the outside world for as long as nine weeks. TV cameras spied on them 24 hours a day, and barbed wire kept out unwelcome visitors!*

IN AND OUT

Interactive TV lets viewers feed in choices and information, via the set and phone link, as well as get it out. Flick through the screens of a shopping channel and order goods on the spot.

TELEVISIONS EVERYWHERE

Television in public places has generated debate since the medium began to enter daily life in the late 1940s. The mushrooming alliance between TV and sports (see page 26) led to the idea of the sports bar, with big screens showing live and recorded sports around the world, where friends could watch in a social setting. Another development was the massive replay screens at live events.

Social TV at the local sports bar.

INTERACTIVE TV

In the early '90s a new role for TV was expected to grow hugely – interactive or two-way television. But in 1996 Time Warner's FSN (Full Service Network), the USA's first interactive cable channel, did not pass its two-year trial period. The spread of the Internet meant that on-line interaction by computer, as in shopping, grew faster than the TV version.

THE NET SPREADS

Have you got your own web site? It's a place on the Internet with a unique name. People can visit it using their computers, via the phone network. They see and hear what you have put there. The Internet has grown bigger and faster than any other medium in history.

NETWORKING
Almost every office has computers, not only for accounts or employee details, but to communicate. A company's various computers may link by wires and a device called a server, into a network.

WWW - WOW!
The Internet is the global system of computers joined by the wires and cables, and the microwave, radio and satellite links, of the telecom (phone) network. Parts of the Net are private, such as companies sending information between their offices, or people sending messages by e-mail (electronic mail) to each other. The World Wide Web, or www, is part of the Internet. It's really multimedia – a giant electronic library of words, pictures, sounds, games, animations and much more. Anyone can access it using a computer and phone line.

NETS AND WEBS
The Internet uses the same routes as telephones – the telecommunications network of metal wires, fibreoptic cables, microwave towers and satellite links. Each region has an access point called a gateway, which is like a huge computer – the Net equivalent of a major telephone exchange. The gateway directs messages and information to subnets, which serve smaller areas and route them to their final destinations.

Satellite
Subnet
Gateway
Subnet
Gateway

UNBELIEVABLE GROWTH
In about 1993 there were less than 100 named sites on the World Wide Web. By January '96 the number was 100,000; by April '97 over 1 million. In January 2000 the number of sites rocketed past 10 million – and by the end of the year reached a staggering 25 million. The Internet offers almost anything, from the latest sports or chart music, to the history of origami (paper-folding), to giant shopping malls for buying anything.

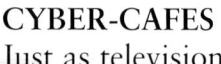

CYBER-CAFES

Just as television screens appeared in cafés and bars (see page 11), so did computer screens linked to the Internet. The cyber-café offered rest, refreshment, and the chance to gather information or simply have fun, alone or with friends. BBC Radio One presenter Steve Lamacq and Dave Rowntree, drummer with chart band Blur, hosted Europe's first live radio show from a cyber-café, with music samples sent in during the show, by listeners via the Internet.

Rowntree (left) and Lamacq at Café Cyberia.

CYBERSPACE

'Cyberspace' is an electronic place – an unreal or virtual world that exists only as tiny electrical pulses in computer circuits. The cyberspace of the Internet presents endlessly flexible multimedia for use by advertisers, businesses, public services such as libraries, shoppers, special interest groups such as bottle-top collectors, and anyone else.

WEB SITES
Sites on the World Wide Web vary from huge companies trying to encourage their business, to individual people having a laugh.

13

ELECTRONIC MAIL
E-mail is similar to a letter sent through the postal service. It goes privately, direct from sender to receiver. But it is sent in seconds, rather than the day or two of post.

UNCONTROLLABLE

By the '90s, tiny microphones and cameras, radio transmitters and other gadgets could turn anyone into James Bond. Spying on people and their secrets was easy. But was it legal, and even if it was, should it be done at all?

RIGHT TO PRIVACY

Hidden 'bug' microphones, remote-control cameras, and phone or computer 'taps' are the modern equivalent of peeking through a keyhole. Like real spies and private detectives, the media's journalists, photographers and reporters sometimes use undercover methods which are legally doubtful. If this exposes serious crime and corruption, most people agree it is justified. But what if it invades a person's private life, and causes grievous upset, just to sell more newspapers or boost TV ratings?

SPY IN THE SKY

Rotors powered by quiet electric motor

Battery pack

Small stills or video camera

Radio control receiver

Microphone

A model radio-controlled helicopter makes a sneaky 'spy' to take photos with an on-board camera. The pictures can be sent as they are taken, by radio to a receiver, in case the craft is captured or damaged. Such cameras have many worthwhile uses, like surveying dangerous crash scenes. Their use in the media is much more controversial.

JUST AN ORDINARY DAY
Almost every day Diana, Princess of Wales was subjected to intense media scrutiny. Photographers swarmed around her for all kinds of pictures. Ordinary life is impossible under such relentlessly stressful conditions.

WHAT WE WANT?
The paparazzi *are photographers who use almost any trick to get an unusual or desirable picture, to sell to the highest bidder. Their methods often cause the public to throw up their hands in horror. But who buys the pictures, so creating the need? The public ...*

LOOKING FOR BLAME

After the death of Diana, everyone asked: 'who was to blame?' Eager as ever to satisfy public demand, the media pounced – on some of its own workers, especially the *paparazzi* (see left). Suddenly roles were reversed. The photographers felt the glare of the media spotlight. They had to justify their involvement and proclaim their innocence in contributing to the fatal car crash.

Photographers under questioning.

THE MOST FAMOUS FACE

The world's best-known, most photographed person of the '90s was probably Diana, Princess of Wales. She married the heir to the British throne, Prince Charles, in 1981. But personal problems led to their separation. Diana was beautiful, fashionable, kind-hearted, and worked tirelessly for the disadvantaged and poor. Yet she was also vulnerable and often unhappy. Her life was a fascinating mixture of success and tragedy, and her face on a magazine or newspaper was bound to increase its sales.

SUDDEN LOSS

In 1997 the world was stunned by Diana's death in a car crash. Accusations flew that the media were to blame. Had a chasing posse of reporters and photographers, who always followed her every move, caused the crash? An enquiry found this was not so. But the event once again highlighted the dangers of excessive media attention.

FARAWAY PHOTOS
Cameras with telephoto lenses can take pictures from far away. Aimed in secret, through hedges or windows, these can make a private life very public. Many complicated laws govern their use.

15

INSTANT NEWS

Tiny cameras, microphones, radios, satellites and other gadgets do not make news by themselves. They need media people. News crews must be on standby, able to rush to an event even as it starts, so that we can watch and listen 'live as it happens'.

POWER OF TV

In June 1994, an instant-news event showed TV's ever-increasing power. US football and screen star O.J. Simpson had been charged with killing his former wife Nicole and her friend. But Simpson went missing. Then a friend contacted police to say that he and O.J. were driving across Los Angeles on a main road – and Simpson was threatening suicide.

TV VERSUS PRESS
TV reports are fast but fleeting. For in-depth study and lasting impressions, people turn to the print media of papers, magazines and books.

ON TRIAL
After the highway chase, O.J. Simpson gave himself up for trial, defended by Johnnie Cochran Jr (below). In October '95, the world tuned in again. The verdict: Not guilty.

HOT PURSUIT

TV crews raced to their helicopters. Guided by the friend's information, they located and flew above Simpson in his white truck, weaving through traffic. On-board cameras sent TV pictures by radio signals to a local station, which then 'patched' them into networks. Normal TV was interrupted as millions tuned in to see the drama of cop cars chasing a famous fleeing suspect. It looked just like a movie or TV show – but this was real life!

16

ENOUGH SIGNALS

The basic technology for such instant links was not new. But by the '90s, 'broadband' versions could pack enough coded signals into the available time, to carry TV pictures that change many times each second. By the year 2000, CNN (Cable News Network) was using over 20 satellites and reaching more than 150 million households in 200-plus countries.

WIRED

By the late '90s, information could be sent from a laptop computer, through the telecom system used by phones. This included writing, and also pictures and sounds from a pocket-sized digital camera.

NEWS ONLINE

The Internet began to change news-consuming habits. As more computers came online, users could switch conveniently from normal work on screen, briefly to check events on a news web site. Employers argued that this was an abuse of company time and equipment. Employees argued that it was similar to listening to news headlines on an office radio.

Make news or take news – the Internet could do both.

RUSH TO THE SCENE

As big news happened, TV and radio stations raced to get people and equipment there. Trucks, cars, even motorcycles acted as small, mobile ground stations, their dishes accurately aligned to beam signals to satellites high in space.

STORED FOREVER

The 20th century began with the medium of recorded sound stored as a wavy groove in a gramophone disc. It ended with MP3, the all-electronic format for computers and the Internet. But other formats, which appeared in between, were still thriving.

DISC-MAD WORLD

The '80s had brought CDs, compact discs. About 74 minutes of almost perfect sound was stored as a digital code of microscopic pits on a shiny disc, read by a laser beam which could be skipped at once to any part. In the '90s, CD technology was both reduced, and extended to include not only sounds, but pictures.

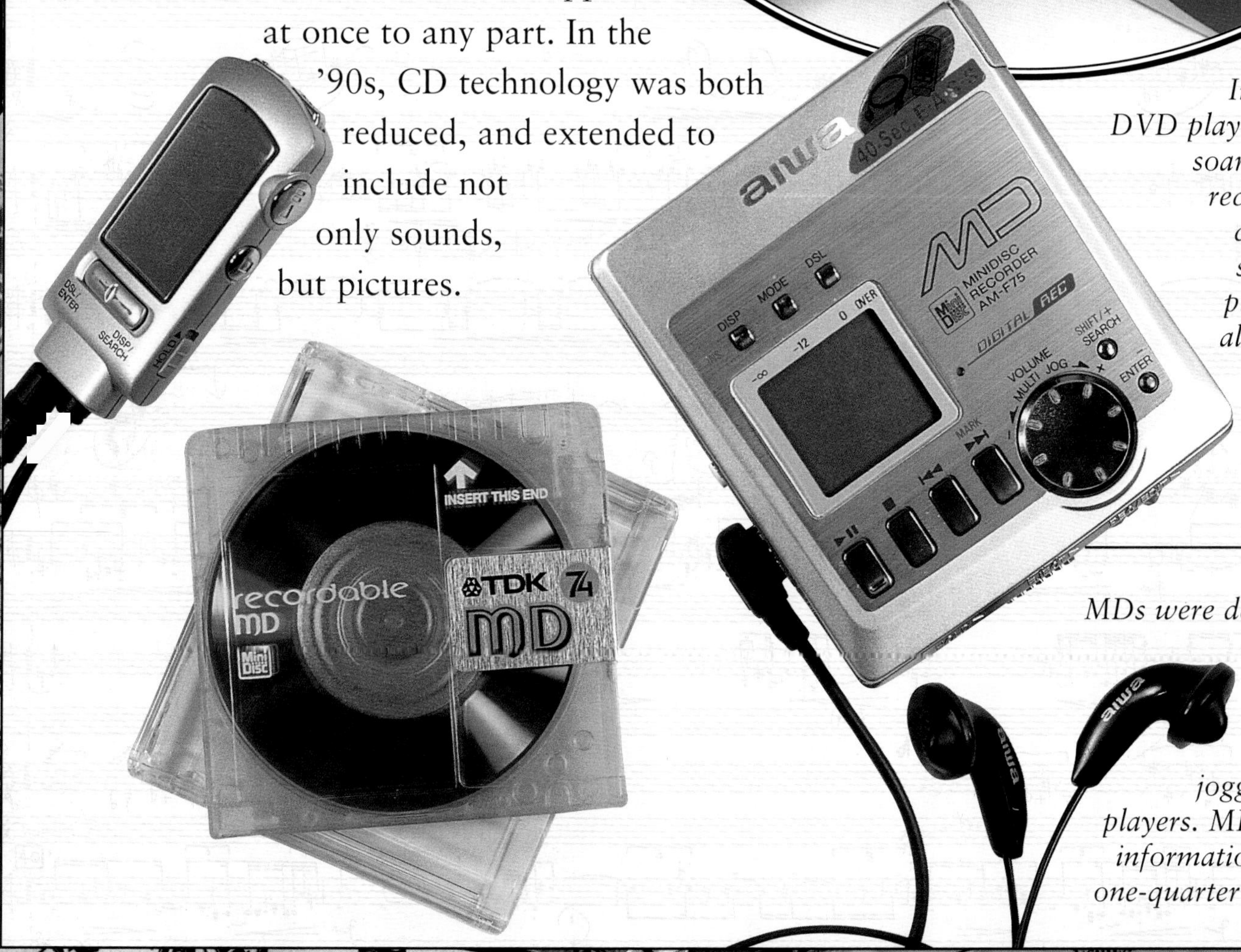

DVD

In the late 1990s DVD player sales began to soar, mainly for pre-recorded movies or collections of TV shows. Domestic players that could also record had to wait until the 2000s.

ML

MDs were designed from the outset to be re-recordable, ultra-convenient and anti-joggable in persona players. MDs hold as much information as CDs but in one-quarter of the disc area

MP3
MP3 audio files can be played on and manipulated by a computer, or fed into a memory 'stick' for use in a domestic MP3 player and music system, or in the tiny personal MP3 player.

COPYRIGHT ON TRIAL

For years, people taped vinyl records or CDs. In practice, this did not interfere greatly with copyright laws, provided it was for personal use only. But putting music on to the Internet made it available to millions – and often for free. The recorded music industry reacted by taking to court organizations such as Napster, that made MP3 files available. The controversy raged into the 2000s.

Representatives of Napster face the media.

LESS, MORE

The reduced version was the MiniDisc, MD, announced by Sony in May 1991. It had the same sound content and quality as a CD, but was only 64 mm across – and you could record and re-record on it. The tiny personal MD player soon became a must-have fashion item. The CD's extended version was the DVD, Digital Versatile Disc. The same size as a CD, it could hold 7–8 times more information – enough for all the images and sounds of a full-length movie, with extras such as the director's comments and out-takes.

MUSIC ONLINE

The no-moving-parts, all-digital-electronic MP3 format was designed specially for sending along telecom lines, as used by the Internet, and storing on a computer disc. MP3 compresses the original files of recorded sounds, so a typical song takes minutes rather than hours to send via Internet or e-mail.

VINYL DISC
Even by 2000, demand still existed for recordings on vinyl disc. Some audio enthusiasts prefer the slight inconsistencies and imperfections, saying that vinyl sounds 'warm and human' while CD formats appear 'cold and impersonal'.

19

VIRTUAL MOVIES

1995 saw a landmark in the medium of cinema – the first feature film generated entirely using computers. It had no real-life actors, no models, no hand-drawn animation. It was virtual.

DIGI-DINOS
A combination of scale models, full-sized robotics, hands-on animation and computer graphics created scaly, scary, cunning stars in Jurassic Park.

TOY STORY
Old-timer Woody, space-age Buzz Lightyear and their toy friends took up as much as a million hours of computer processing time. Toy Story 2 (1999) was another massive hit.

FIRST AMONG EQUALS

Two years earlier new standards in SFX (special effects) had been set by director Steven Spielberg and his team, for the story of dinosaurs recreated in the modern world, *Jurassic Park*. Some of the trickiest scenes featured interactions between the real-life actors and the modelled, computerized or animated dinosaurs. This interplay of real and virtual was a problem that *Toy Story* did not face.

BOX-OFFICE BIGGIES

Both films were smash hits, and not only for their ground-breaking SFX. They were promoted by a blitz of adverts, and a vast array of toys, games, theme meals and spin-off merchandise. Also, satisfied movie-goers thought that the films had strong storylines, humour, tension, drama, sadness and a happy ending – the classic ingredients of fine cinema. Many other 'firsts' in the medium of movies have passed by more quietly, because the films themselves were less memorable.

Luton Sixth Form College

BACK TO THE FUTURE

A final '90s blockbuster promised much. *Star Wars 1: The Phantom Menace* was the first episode of the cosmically successful space saga that began in 1977. The film had wall-to-wall adverts, dazzling SFX and endless merchandise. Yet it failed to capture the magic of the original.

CGI DINOSAURS

Computer-generated imagery (CGI) begins with a 'map' of an object in the computer, using points in three dimensions – height, breadth and depth. The map may come originally from a life-size model. The points are linked in the computer by maths equations, which allow them to move in relation to each other, but only within certain limits.

Contour lines join ma points to give impression of overall covering (dinosaur skin)

Movement of leg also causes skin along flank to 'stretch'

21

TITANIC
The most expensive movie to make, at $200 million plus, Titanic (1997) captivated viewers with its special effects. A vast life-sized mock-up of one side of the ship was constructed. For views of the other side, the film was flipped (turned left to right), and the crew wore hats with reversed 'mirror' writing.

THE MEDIA ON THE MEDIA
In *The Truman Show* (1998), Jim Carrey plays Truman Burbank, who thinks he leads a normal life. In fact, from birth he has existed in a giant TV set. His family and friends are actors, and the rest of the world tunes into watch – the ultimate 'reality TV' (see page 11). The movie is a powerful comment on such media manipulation.

IT COULD HAPPEN TO YOU!

Truman suspects someone is watching – indeed, everyone is.

WORLD CINEMA

Almost no mass-market movie of the '90s, made by the industrialized Western nations, was safe from computerized special effects. But away from space and science-fiction blockbusters, there were many other cinema trends around the world.

'BOLLYWOOD'

The biggest centre for making feature films was not Hollywood, USA, but 'Bollywood'. This is the nickname given to India's hugely prolific and successful film industry. Throughout the '90s it regularly produced 800–900 movies per year, in more than a dozen languages including Hindi, Bengali, Gujarati and Tamil. Biggest earner of the decade was *Hum Aapke Hain Kaun* (1994), starring Bollywood's leading actor Shah Rukh Khan and actress Madhuri Dixit. Each could command half a million-plus dollars per project.

HISTORY REPEATS ITSELF

Gripping drama adapted from history still scooped awards. In '93, cinema's top honour, Oscar for Best Picture, went to a harrowing tale of Nazi Germany, *Schindler's List*, and in '96, to a portrayal of Scottish freedom-fighter William Wallace in *Braveheart*.

'THIS AIN'T NO GAME!'
A new trend saw movies adapted from video or computer games. Characters and plots were already familiar from playing the game. An early example involved reptile-fighting plumbers Super Mario Brothers *(1993).*

EVIL OF THE HOLOCAUST

Director Steven Spielberg had made not one, but seven of the all-time biggest movies. First formal recognition of his work came with not one, but seven Oscars for Schindler's List, *with terrifying scenes of Nazi persecution of Jews in the 1940s.*

The Blair Witch Project *was directed by Daniel Myrick and Eduardo Sanchez.*

SCARY EARNINGS

By far the biggest-earning film compared to its cost was the apparently real horror tale, *The Blair Witch Project* (1999). Estimates of its budget vary from $22,000 to $100,000 – about one day's food expenses for a big Hollywood movie. Yet in just a year *Blair* took more than $140 million at the box office. It was promoted on the Internet, by word of mouth and in a few specialist magazines, adding to its spooky secrecy and 'underground' appeal.

THRILLS 'N' SPILLS

All-action thrillers, often with equal portions of drama, humour, suspense and horror, were huge hits, including *Speed* (1994) and its sequels, and *Scream* (1996) and its sequels. And no decade since the '60s was complete without superspy James Bond, in the most profitable film series ever. He ended the millennium with *The World Is Not Enough* (1999).

'FREEDOM!'

Fighting for his nation's independence, heroic Wallace's rallying cry in 13th-century Scotland actually came from the mouth of Australian star Mel Gibson. Mel won an Oscar for best director.

INDIAN EPICS

'Bollywood' often featured traditional plots. Boy meets girl, boy loses girl, boy triumphs over adversity and wins girl, happy ending – often with songs.

MUSIC AND MOVIES
Natalie Appleton and Mel Blatt, of R&B and hip-hop influenced All Saints, accept a music video award. The media of movies and music videos shared many common styles.

MUSICAL DREAMS

The medium of popular music largely played safe during the '90s. Dozens of already established styles continued, from heavy metal and progressive rock, to gangsta rap and hip hop, to mass-market, sugar-coated pop. But two new trends also hit the headlines.

BRITPOP

From about 1994, music journalists began to mention 'Britpop'. It referred to guitar-based bands playing lively songs of English character, with catchy tunes, and without the 'rock-god' posturing and screaming guitar solos of US-based, stadium-sized superstars such as Bon Jovi, Van Halen and Aerosmith.

LOTZA AWARDS
Blur are honoured at a major UK music event, the Brit Awards, in 'Britpop year' 1995. The numbers of awards grew steadily, with Grammys, MTVs, MOJOs, MOBOs, BBCs, Q Magazines, Billboards, NMEs...

LEADERZ OF THE PACK

Britpop 'pack leaders' were Suede with the album *Suede* (1993), Blur with *Parklife* ('94), Pulp with *Different Class* ('95), and the swearing, argumentative, often drunk-and-violent Oasis, with their phenomenally successful albums *Definitely Maybe* ('94) and *(What's the Story) Morning Glory?* ('95). But in the fickle world of modern music, by the late '90s Britpop was no longer new, and so less popular.

THE RISKY BANDWAGON

Popular music's huge influence drew people hoping to gain 'street cred' by being seen with the latest stars. However, the ploy could backfire. At the '98 Brit Awards, a member of very Socialist Liverpool band Chumbawamba poured water over British Labour Party politician John Prescott.

Prescott got a dousing.

MUSIC ON TV
The media of television and popular music continued to feed off each other, with dedicated music channel·MTV leading the way.

BOYZ AND GIRLZ

A second trend was the boy- or girl-band. Some could sing a bit, dance after a fashion, perhaps play an instrument – but all were groomed for multimedia consumption by an ever-younger audience. British examples included Take That, Boyzone, Spice Girls and All Saints. When Take That split in '96, special phone helplines were swamped by tearful girls. From their ashes rose the pop superstar of the late '90s – Robbie Williams.

25

GIRL POWER
The Spice Girls burst on to the pop music scene in 1996 with Wannabe. *Four years later they were pursuing solo careers.*

BIGGEST SELLER
Following Diana's death (see page 15), Elton John's new version of his Candle in the Wind *became the biggest selling record ever, over 30 million in 37 days.*

MEDIA MEET SPORT

A major growth area for the media involved their links with sports. Players and competitors swelled the growing army of presenters, commentators, analyzers and summarizers for TV, video, radio, books and magazines.

SPORTS ON THE SET

More than ever, sports events were organized around television coverage – especially under pressure from advertisers.

International soccer matches in Asia began very late at night, to catch the sport's main market of early-evening viewers in Europe. In Britain, the adverts-free BBC lost several major sports, such as Formula One motor racing and International Test-Match Cricket, to commercial channels such as ITV and Sky. They could afford to bid much larger sums for broadcasting rights.

26

IS IT SPORT?
WWF, World Wrestling Federation, brought the 'grapple game' back to the big time with glitz and glamour.

GOOD AND BAD
In 1999, Michael Jordan retired (again) as basketball's greatest. 'Bad boy' Dennis Rodman was famous for his infamous reputation.

TELEVISUAL FEAST
The Soccer World Cup in France in 1998, and the Olympic Games in Sydney in 2000, were the decade's most complex televised events. Even a standard league match, like soccer, demanded a huge TV crew and dozens of cameras.

JORDAN
23

HELP OR HINDRANCE?

The increasing technology of media coverage, especially TV, led to problems in some sports. Slow-motion replays became so common that incidents could be shown several times within seconds, undermining the judgement and authority of referees and umpires. But some sports, such as baseball, rugby and cricket, turned this to advantage. They allowed referees and umpires to ask for the opinions of colleagues with access to TV replay.

'It was out.' 'No, in.' 'Out!' 'In!'

PROBLEM ADS

Many governments banned advertising sponsorship by alcohol and tobacco companies. Impressionable young people might be exposed to such adverts.

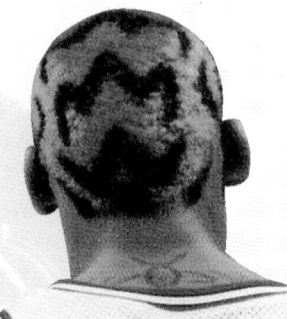

HOT MEDIA PROPERTY

Stars were hot property. German Formula One race ace Michael Schumacher, US golf phenomenon Tiger Woods, basketball greats Michael Jordan and Shaquille O'Neal, and Brazil's soccer wizard Renaldo got paid more in a month than many people earned in a lifetime.

MEDIA DREAM

Some stars earned more outside their sport, in the media, than within it. They did TV and radio interviews, put their names to columns for newspapers and magazines, presented videos, and of course, showed advertisers' names and symbols on their clothing and equipment. In 1999, the heady worlds of sports and pop music collided as Manchester United and England soccer star David Beckham married Victoria 'Posh Spice' Adams of the Spice Girls. A royal wedding could hardly attract more attention. 'Posh 'n' Becks' became the dream couple for media and advertising.

INTO THE NEW MILLENNIUM

Looking back at the media in 1900, there were books, newspapers, posters, visual arts like photography, painting and sculpture, and live performance. Sound recording and movies were in their infancy, and radio was experimental. Who was brave enough to predict the future?

Y2K bug hits cash dispensers in Japan.

MEDIA TAKE-OVER

Even in 1950 there was little TV, no magnetic tapes or compact discs, and of course, no computers or Internet. Just 50 years later, the media have changed beyond recognition. Not only in their technology, such as thumb-sized digital cameras and Internet-ready mobile phones, but also in the media's ever-increasing involvement in daily life.

MILLENNIUM
The Year 2000 celebrations were a gigantic media-fest. Australia's Sydney Harbour Bridge became the world's biggest fireworks-holder.

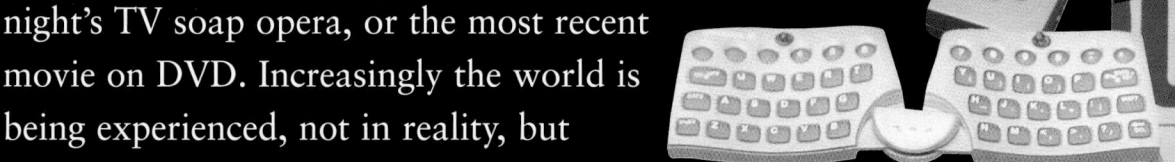

ELECTRO-WARNING

Not only the media, but also business, industry, travel, even education, increasingly rely on computerized electronic systems. Various Y2K (Year 2000) computer 'bugs' threatened global disruption, but most failed to have an impact. However, if such a bug affected the news media, people could not be warned about it or how to prepare for it.

MEDIA MANIPULATION

For many people, everyday chat is no longer about business news, or a scientific invention, or even the weather. It's more likely to be about the newest pop music star's clothes, last night's TV soap opera, or the most recent movie on DVD. Increasingly the world is being experienced, not in reality, but through the pictures and words of the media. Can we trust them to present an honest, truthful version? Or do they manipulate what we see, hear and feel, for their own ends?

GADGETS GALORE
Internet videophones, palm-sized supercomputers and flexible foldaway screens are some of the media-led products under development.

MEDIA FUTURE

The media hold unique positions of influence and power. They inform, entertain and comfort us. But they can also change our opinions and persuade us – maybe to depend on them, even more than we do now. Amazing changes have occurred at ever-increasing speed through the last century. One prediction seems certain. The media will change even more, and even faster, in the next.

CURLING UP IN BED ...

… With a good book is an age-old tradition. Multimedia could bring an electronic book, with pages that turn like real paper. But they are flexi-screens. They show words and pictures from a pea-sized memory chip. The pictures could be moving or animated, with sounds too, for being sung to sleep.

Complex as a computer, convenient as a paperback book.

29

PRINT ALIVE!
When computers spread during the 1970s, some people believed that the printed media would fade and die. But more book titles are published today than ever before.

TIMES PAST AND PRESENT
News-gathering methods today would baffle year 1900 reporters. Like then, the headlines usually contain bad news. But 'serious' news is often replaced by showbiz gossip – showbiz sells.

GLOSSARY

BROADCAST MEDIA News and information sent out to many people – that is, broadcast – usually in the form of radio (electromagnetic) waves, as radio and TV programmes.

CABLE In telecommunications and media technology, a bundle of hair-thin fibre-optic strands that carry information in the form of coded pulses of laser light.

CD Compact disc, a format for storing information or data (pictures, words, sounds, computer programs and more) as microscopic pits on the shiny surface of a small or 'compact' disc.

DIGITAL A system that uses numbers or digits (usually 0 and 1) as separate or 'discontinuous' units, to code for information. The contrasting analogue system uses continuously varying up-and-down quantities or waves.

DVD Digital versatile disc, a format for storing information or data (pictures, words, sounds, animations, computer programs and more) as microscopic pits on the shiny surface of a small or 'compact' disc. DVDs hold 7–8 times more information than CDs.

PRINT MEDIA News and information printed or otherwise put on to paper, as in books, magazines, journals, newspapers and posters.

RADIO The general name for the sound-only medium which uses invisible electromagnetic waves sent out, or broadcast, from transmitter to receiver. 'A radio' is also the everyday name for a radio receiver or radio set.

REALITY TV When television spies on or records the activities of people who are supposedly acting naturally, without acting or interference from cameras, presenters and interviewers. Similar to the 'fly-on-the-wall' television techniques used for documentaries. The best-known reality TV programme is *Big Brother*, which originated in The Netherlands.

VIDEO Term with several meanings, based around moving pictures as stored on magnetic tape (videotape) or CD/DVD, in contrast to moving pictures as recorded on photographic film (as for the cinema). Also used as a nickname for the machine called the VCR, video-cassette recorder-player.

30

WORLD EVENTS

- Iraq invades Kuwait, Gulf War ensues

- South Africa: Nelson Mandela freed from jail

- USSR finally breaks up

- Civil war looms in Yugoslavia

- Somalia devastated by war and famine

- USA: Race riots in Los Angeles

- Europe: Bosnia-Herzegovina atrocities

- Bill Clinton becomes President of USA

- South Africa: First all-race elections, Mandela appointed President

- USA: Terrorist bomb in Oklahoma City

- Japan: Nerve gas attacks, Tokyo subway

- Afghanistan: Taliban Muslims seize power

- UK: 'Mad cow disease' BSE fears

- Hong Kong comes under Chinese control

- UK: Tony Blair becomes prime minister

- Europe: Euro unit of currency begins

- India and Pakistan debate nuclear tests

- Russia: Vladimir Putin becomes President

TIMELINE

HEADLINES	MEDIA EVENTS	MEDIA TECH	PERFORMANCE & ART
•*Geneva: World Climate Conference warns of global warming*	•*Mandela tribute concert at Wembley, London* •*Grunge music appears with Nirvana*	•*Robots get their own Olympics, Scotland*	•*Madonna's best-of* The Immaculate Collection •*Spooky-funny movie* Edward Scissorhands
•*Boris Yeltzin becomes Russian leader*	•*Sony launches re-recordable MiniDisc* •*UK: Bryan Adams has longest-ever No. 1 single*	•*Whole encyclopedia put on to pocket computer*	•*Girls on the road with* Thelma and Louise •*Jostein Gaarder:* Sophie's World
•*Rio de Janeiro: 'Last Chance' environmental summit*	•*Queen's Freddie Mercury AIDS awareness concert*	•*First videophones go into testing* •*Digital compact cassette, DCC*	•*Jungle music hits hard* •*Olivier Messiaen dies*
•*Palestine Liberation Organization and Israel: first of many accords*	•*Schindler's List at last wins Oscars for Spielberg* •*Oasis gains popularity*	•*Electronic notepads with pen-sensing screens recognize handwriting*	•*Jurassic Park movie sets new standards for SFX* •*Icelandic singer-writer Björk's Debut album*
•*Los Angeles: O. J. Simpson car chase* •*Rwanda: Civil war and genocide*	•*Europe: Channel Tunnel opens* •*Nirvana's 'grunge' leader Kurt Cobain's suicide*	•*Number of Internet subscribers breaks 30 million*	•*Aaron computer program develops its own art style* •*Quentin Tarrantino's cult movie Pulp Fiction*
•*Japan: City of Kobe destroyed by earthquake* •*Israeli leader Yitzak Rabin assassinated*	•*Freeplay battery-free wind-up radio launched* •*O. J. Simpson receives verdict: innocent*	•*Toy Story is the first feature movie generated entirely on computer*	•*'Britpop' year as UK pop groups succeed worldwide* •*Installationist Christo wraps Berlin's Reichstag*
•*'Alien fossil microbes' found in a meteorite from Mars are eventually revealed to be crystals*	•*USA: Two-year Time Warner interactive cable TV experiment ends* •*Philips offers Web TV*	•*Number of Internet subscribers breaks 50 million* •*Nikon E2 digital camera*	• *UK: Take That boy band splits up* •*UK: Spice Girls girl band hits the top of the charts*
•*Diana, Princess of Wales, and Dodi Fayed die in car crash, Paris*	•*Dolly the Sheep generates endless cloning debates in the media*	•*Internet web sites exceed 1 million* •*DVDs launched to lukewarm reception*	•*Titanic becomes the most expensive movie ever made* •*Elton John's Diana tribute song is fastest-seller ever*
•*Frank Sinatra, voted 'century's most popular singer', dies*	•*Soccer World Cup in France is most complex televised event ever*	•*Apple iMac range quickly taken up for Internet use, web / printed page design* •*MP3s become common*	•*The media lampoon themselves in Jim Carrey's* The Truman Show
•*Christian / Western World prepares for the Millennium – greatest-ever multimedia festival*	•*UK: Marriage of 'Posh 'n' Becks', soccer star David Beckham and Spice Girl Victoria Adams*	•*Internet web sites pass 20 million* •*Pokemon cartoons and games are the new craze*	•Star Wars 1: The Phantom Menace *is hyped* •The Blair Witch Project *is not hyped*

INDEX

Adams, Victoria 27
advertising 13, 27
Aerosmith 24
All Saints 24, 25
analogue 8, 9, 10
ANC 6–7
animation 20
apartheid 6–7
Apple computers 9
Appleton, Natalie 24
awards, music 24

BBC 10, 13, 27
Beckham, David 27
Big Brother 11
binary digits (bits) 8
Blair Witch Project 23
Blatt, Mel 24
Blur 13, 24
Bollywood 22–23
Bon Jovi 24
Bond, James 14, 23
books 5, 28
boy bands 25
Boyzone 25
Britpop 24
broadband 17
BSkyB 10
bugs, computer 29

cable TV 4
cameras 14, 16, 17
capacity 10
Carrey, Jim 21
CCTV (Chinese TV) 10
CDs 4, 8, 9, 18, 19
CGI 21
Charles, Prince 15
China 10
chips, micro- 9
Chumbawamba 25
cinema 22–23
CNN 17
Cochran, Johnnie, Jr 16
computers 4, 8–9, 12,
    17, 19, 20, 21, 22, 29
computer images 20–21

copyright 19
cyber-cafés 13
cyberspace 13

decoders 8
de Klerk, F. W. 7
Diana, Princess 14, 25
digital systems 5, 8–9,
    10, 17, 18, 28
Dixit, Madhuri 22
DVDs 4, 8, 10, 18, 29

e-mail 12, 13, 19

flat screens 9
flexi-screens 29

gangsta rap 24
gateway 12
Gibson, Mel 23
girl bands 25
gramophone 18
ground station 17

heavy metal 24
hip hop 24
Hollywood 22
*Hum Aapke Hain
    Kaun* 22

iMac computer 9
Indian film industry 22
interactive TV 10–11
Internet 4, 5, 12, 17–19,
    23, 28–29
ITV 10, 27

Japan 29
John, Elton 25
Jordan, Michael 26, 27
journalists 4
Jurassic Park 20

Khan, Shah Rukh 22

Lamacq, Steve 13
Los Angeles 16

Mandela, Nelson 6–7
manipulation 21, 29
mass media 5
merchandise 20
microphones 14, 16
millennium 28
MiniDisc (MD) 18–19
movies 4, 5, 10, 20–23
MP3 18, 19
MTV 25
multimedia 12, 25, 29
Myrick, Daniel 23

Napster 19
Nazis 22, 23
New York Tribune 29
news gathering 16, 29

Oasis 24
Olympic Games 27
O'Neal, Shaquille 27
Oscar awards 22–23

paparazzi 15
PDAs 9
Phantom Menace 21
photography 14, 15
popular music 24–25
Prescott, John 25
print media 5, 27, 29
privacy 14–15

radio 4, 8
rap 24
reality TV 11, 21
Renaldo 27
replays, slow-motion 27
rock, progressive 24
Rodman, Dennis 26
Rowntree, Dave 13

Sanchez, Eduardo 23
satellites 10, 17, 20
Schindler's List 22–23
Schumacher, Michael 27
Scream 23
shopping channels 11

Simpson, O. J. 16
Sky 27
soap operas 29
Soccer World Cup 27
sound, recorded 18–19
South Africa 6–7
special effects 20–21, 22
Speed 23
Spice Girls 25, 27
Spielberg, Steven 20, 23
sports 10, 11, 26–27
spying 14
Star Wars 21
subnet 12
Suede 24
Super Mario Brothers 22

Take That 25
Tarrant, Chris 10
telecoms 12, 17, 19
telephoto lenses 15
television 4, 8, 10, 11,
    16–17, 21, 26–27
terrorism 6
text messages 5
The Times 29
*The World Is Not
    Enough* 23
Time Warner 11
Titanic 21
Toy Story 20
Truman Show 21

Van Halen 24
video 10
videophone 29
vinyl disc 19
virtual technology 20

Wallace, William 22–23
web sites 12, 13
Wembley 7
Williams, Robbie 25
Woods, Tiger 27
World Wide Web 12
World Wrestling
    Federation 26

32